The TOTAL MAN

By Dr. Lester Sumrall

Unless otherwise indicated,
all Scripture quotations are taken from
the *King James Version* of the Bible.

The Total Man
ISBN 0-937580-34-1
Copyright © 1984 by
Lester Sumrall Evangelistic Association
Published by LESEA Publishing Company
P.O. Box 12
South Bend, Indiana 46624

3rd printing, 1985
Over 100,000 in print

Contents

INTRODUCTION

This is a series of four books packaged together for your convenience, you can also purchase any of the four volumes separately.

This volume describes the unity of the human personality. It shows how the three distinct parts of the human person function in harmony.

An automobile has 14,000 different parts. When they all perform in unity you have soft and pleasurable transportation.

When your total person is united in oneness with God you are happy, resourceful, and delight in sharing your success with others.

I have been more than twenty years studying the subject of the dividing or separating the human spirit and the human soul. In my search for truth I found little material on the subject. But of recent years there have appeared books and magazine articles on the subject.

It may not be possible to live a victorious and fulfilling life without pertinent knowledge of the total man, spirit, soul, and body.

1

THE NEW THING

The great Psalmist said in Psalm 8:4, "What is man, that thou art mindful of him? and the son of man, that thou visitest him?"

Evidently the Psalmist suddenly became alarmed by the immensity of this thing called man. For six thousand years this question has been on the lips of humans, "What is man that you are giving such attention to him, God?" The whole of the Bible was written primarily for man. It is not a book on astrology or astronomy. It is not a book on sciences; it is a book about man.

Possibly there is no truth whose time has so

fully come as the truth about the total man.
Maybe there has never been such eagerness
in our land to understand this truth as there is
at this moment. I am very delighted for this.
This truth can resolve personal problems; it
can resolve family problems, church problems, and resolve community problems.
When we get to know the truth of the total
man, we get to the very core and center of all
human problems. It is not enough to have a
definition; we must have an application of
how this truth works and then it is really useful
to us.

There are only three major areas of educa-
tion with which all of us must grapple.

WHO IS GOD?

The first and primary area is God. A person
who does not know God has not actually
started to live. How can a person say he
knows how to live if he does not know God? I
am a firm believer that God made this earth,
and we ought to know something about Him.
When you see a watch, wouldn't you like to
know the maker? Have you ever wondered
how God makes humans? The greatest
knowledge that a human can get in this world

is a knowledge of God. Very few people ever get to know God. Many people know about God, but they do not know God. If you are not willing to concentrate and penetrate and to seek with your total being to know God, you will not know Him.

The greatest revelation of God is in the Bible and you should begin at the first page and read to the last page. What a study you would enjoy!

Atheists, communists, or agnostics do not know God! Sinners do not know God either! Yet we do not really live until we begin to know God. To know Him is to understand what life is all about. God was so desirous that we get to know Him, that He sent His son to represent Him so that in the Son we would see God. John 3:16 says, "For God so loved the world, that he gave his only begotten Son, that whosoever believeth in him should not perish, but have everlasting life."

KNOW YOUR FELLOWMAN

The second vast area of information for every human to know is knowing our fellowman. It is amazing that we can live with humans all our lives and not know anything about them. Have you ever heard a man say after living with a woman for fifty years, "I don't understand you"? He thought that he did when he married her but somewhere along the line the communications broke down.

We would not have wars if we knew one another. The Russians are nice people; I have lived with them. The Germans are lovely people; I have lived with them too. All nations are full of nice people. If we had a knowledge of one another there would not be wars or any other kind of friction. If there was a complete understanding between management and labor there would not be all the friction we have. It is an understanding of our fellowman that we need, but so many times we do not seek for that understanding. We do not try to see what makes this person hurt, or what makes that person sad, or what makes the other person feel that we do not care for him. We do not seek to understand what makes others happy or unhappy. Until we know who God is and learn to understand our fellowman, we have not started to live.

KNOW YOURSELF

The third great key to understanding successful living is to know yourself. Very few humans know themselves at all. I struggled honestly and sincerely and continually for more than twenty years to understand the difference between spirit and soul. I asked almost every prominent religious leader that I met in my travels throughout the whole world. As soon as I would meet a Biblical scholar I would say, "What is the spirit of a human? Where does it reside? How does it manifest itself? When does a person receive his spirit—at birth or rebirth?"

Do you know I could not find a single person that could tell me. Finally, the answer came by revelation.

YOUR SPIRIT— THE BORN AGAIN NATURE

One morning, about two o'clock, I was begging God to tell me. God spoke very beautifully to me and said, "Your spirit is your born-again nature."

I replied, "That sounds very simple." Then suddenly the whole great truth bubbled and burst open right in my face and I began to explain it to others in campmeetings and con-

ventions all over this country. I began to talk
about this total man. Who he is and what he is
have become very common subjects today,
but I had never heard one sermon on it for the
first thirty years of my ministry.

David asked in Psalm 8:4-6, "What is
man, that thou are mindful of him? and the
son of man, that thou visitest him? For thou
hast made him a little lower than the angels,
and hast crowned him with glory and honour.
Thou madest him to have dominion over the
works of thy hands; thou hast put all things
under his feet."

MAN'S COMPOSITE NATURE

I had read that Scripture dozens of times,
and didn't see it until God told me what the
composite nature of a human person really is.
I read it dozens of times, but its meaning did
not come to me until God showed me that
your spirit and your soul are distinctly different. Suddenly I understood what God
meant when He said, "I crowned man with
glory and honor." Man has dominion over
the works of God's hands. This means that
we, as humans, have dominion. God has put
all things under our feet. Would it not be
wonderful if we lived up to all the things that
belong to us?

Hebrews 4:12 says, "For the word of God is quick, (the old English word "quick" does not mean "fast;" it means "moving" or "living") and powerful, and sharper than any two-edged sword, piercing even to the dividing asunder of soul and spirit..."

If we are ever going to know the difference between our soul and spirit, that knowledge will come from the Word of God. We can study all the psychology in the universities of the world and not come up with an answer because God says His Word has the answer.

If we do not get our answer from the Bible, we will be without an answer for the rest of our lives.

I Thessalonians 5:23 says, "And the very God of peace sanctify you wholly; and I pray God your whole spirit and soul and body be preserved blameless unto the coming of our Lord Jesus Christ."

Outside of the Bible, man is called a dualism or two part creature.

Psychiatry, psychology, and philosophy say that man is two parts. They think he is inside and outside, topside and bottomside. The Word of God says that man is three.

I really feel that God is doing a new thing in our earth today in a remarkable and wonderful way. God is exploding revelation in this end time. This truth has not been fully taught in our generation.

HISTORICAL TRUTH AND PERTINENT TRUTH

There are two embodiments of truth. One of these truths we would call historical truth and the other we would call pertinent truth. We should have a thorough comprehension of this.

Historic truth is unrelated to your destiny. For example, once there was a man named Noah who built a big boat. Noah was not a shipbuilder, but God taught him how to build a boat and even gave him the blueprints for it. Until 1850 A.D. nobody ever built a boat as big as his. We accept this story as history, but it has nothing to do with the peace that is in our hearts now. It has nothing to do with the joy that is in our soul right now. It is true, but it is historic truth.

Pertinent truth is the opposite of that. It has to do with the fact that God loves you, that God gave His Son for you, and that you can be saved right now forever!

There are literally worlds of *pertinent truth* in the Bible that have to do with your joy, happiness, and peace. The doctrine of the total man belongs in the column of pertinent truth. You must understand yourself to be a successful Christian. You have to know who you are before you can direct yourself. It is possible that 95% of all the Christians in our land (even though they are born again and their spirits are alive) still live, act, and think in their Adamic nature and are living in the old man. Within them abides the secret of the new man, but because they have not been taught pertinent truth, they are living in the ways and the feelings of the old Adamic nature. God is now calling them to a new life in Christ Jesus. This is why I want to lead you into the exploration of the third great area of truth, the understanding of ourselves—the total man.

2

THE NEW MAN

In my personal ministry I seek to give almost all of my total time to *pertinent truth*. I feel that my life has been called of God. I am called to dig deep within our personal beings for vital truth that will help you be a better person today. My calling is to show you how to live a victorious life.

In an airport in New York City, while I was waiting for a plane, I was looking through the book department. There I saw a book on *How To Be A Carpenter*. I cannot saw a straight line or screw a screw, so I did not buy that book. Next I found *How To Be A Cook*. I cannot cook either, so I did not buy that one. As I looked I thought, "Isn't it amazing?

Here are books on how to do all these things, except one thing is missing—that is, how to live!" I said, "Wait a minute! They have missed the big one, HOW DO YOU LIVE?" God said, "That is your job!" In these studies I am going to help you understand yourself and therefore know how to live. I want to make you aware of the three-dimensional nature of the human personality. As long as you treat the human personality as a dualism, you will never discover him. A psychologist or psychiatrist might be able to pick you to pieces, but he will not know how to put you back together again. He thinks that the whole of the inner being is soul and he does not even know that man has a spirit. This is a very sad situation because man's biggest problems are in the spirit. Doctors have not yet discovered that dimension.

IN THE LIKENESS OF GOD

God's first words about the total man are in the first chapter of the Bible. Genesis 1:26, "And God said, Let us make man in our image, after our likeness..." When you see God, He will be about your size, He will have two eyes, one nose, two ears, and four fingers and a thumb. In his earthly life, Jesus was totally average and normal. When you get to heaven, the Bible says you will be like Jesus and that we are made in His image and likeness. God was afraid you would not catch it the first time, so He said it twice.

MAN IS CREATED TO RULE

Then God said in Genesis 1:26, "...and let them have dominion." Now maybe the greatest truth that I am going to teach you about this total man is your powerful relationship to this earth. We actually own this earth, yet we bargained it away to the devil. This earth is ours, and in the millennial kingdom we are to rule on this earth just like Adam ruled. He lost it, but Jesus is going to give it back to us. Man is a dominion person. Every man is a king and every woman is a queen on the face of this earth. God made man to have dominion and he made him like Himself—in three parts. God is the sovereign of this total universe and his eternal wisdom conceived the desire to create an intellectual, soulical creature of moral responsibility and integrity.

GOD HAS A PERSONAL SPIRIT

God has been called a spirit, and He is a spirit. God's spirit was active in the creation. The Bible says that the spirit of God moved upon the waters. We find His spirit in redemption. John 3:16 says, "For God so loved the world, that he gave his only begotten Son, that whosoever believeth in him should not perish, but have everlasting life." We find His spirit functioning in that relationship. He communicated with Noah, saying that there would be a flood. He communicated with Abraham. He communicated with Paul and John. It was through His spirit that He communicated Himself to them.

GOD, THE FATHER, HAS A SOUL

This is the divine soul of perfection, never tainted with sin, and never clouded by doubt. His mind is greater than all human comprehension ever has been or ever will be. His emotions are evident in the Scriptures. He has joy, and He has anger. He has every emotion that you find in a human person. God's emotions are never out of place or wrongly used. Rather they are divinely used from His own life. God, in His soulical parts, identifies Himself with man in that He has a mind, emotion, and will.

GOD HAS A BODY

God's body is very likely about the same size as Jesus' body. When Stephen saw Jesus standing beside the Father, he described the scene as though they were natural together. He did not say that the Father was a giant compared to His Son. Acts 7:56-57 says, "...Behold, I see the heavens opened, and the Son of man standing on the right hand of God. Then they cried out with a loud voice, and stopped their ears, and ran upon him with one accord."

God has hands. With His hands He made Adam. *He has eyes to see.* II Chronicles 16:9, "For the eyes of the LORD run to and fro throughout the whole earth, to shew himself strong in the behalf of them whose heart is perfect toward him. . ." *God has a face.* Genesis 32:30, "And Jacob called the name of the place Peniel: for I have seen God face to face, and my life is preserved." He was seen by Moses and the elders in Exodus 24:9-11, "Then went up Moses, and Aaron, Nadab, and Abihu, and seventy of the elders of Israel: And they saw the God of Israel: and there was under his feet as it were a paved work of a sapphire stone, and as it were the body of heaven in his clearness. And upon the nobles of the children of Israel he laid not his hand: also they saw God, and did eat and drink." That is one of the most remarkable scriptures in the whole Bible. Exodus 33:11

says, "And the LORD spake unto Moses face to face, as a man speaketh unto his friend..." Here was a man that saw Him face to face as a friend.

God has fingers. Daniel 5:5, "In the same hour came forth fingers of a man's hand, and wrote over against the candlestick upon the plaster of the wall of the king's palace: and the king saw the part of the hand that wrote." The king saw the hand of God as it wrote. Exodus 31:18, "And he gave unto Moses, when he had made an end of communing with him upon mount Sinai, two tables of testimony, tables of stone, written with the finger of God."

God has feet. He walked with Adam. Genesis 3:8, "And they heard the voice of the LORD God walking in the garden in the cool of the day: and Adam and his wife hid themselves from the presence of the LORD God amongst the trees of the garden."

We find in Genesis 5:22-24 that God walked with Enoch. "And Enoch walked with God after he begat Methuselah three hundred years, and begat sons and daughters: And all the days of Enoch were three hundred sixty and five years: And Enoch walked with God: and he was not; for God took him."

When you and I get to heaven we are going to find that God has a body like we have, and a soul like we have, and a spirit like we have. God made us in His own likeness and His own image. That is precisely the truth. We will understand it all much better when we see Him face to face. Until that time, we accept the Word of God as it is.

Many people think that God is a floating cloud or a ghost or something like vapor coming out of a kettle. But God is like us, when we see God, we are going to see that He has the same wholeness and total man that we have.

God has a voice. Matthew 3:17, "And lo a voice from heaven, saying, This is my beloved Son, in whom I am well pleased." So we find that God's voice was heard by many people. They were all standing around there, and all heard the voice of God speaking and pointing toward Jesus, "This is my beloved Son in whom I am well pleased." We read in Exodus 33:23, "And I will take away mine hand, and thou shalt see my back parts: but my face shall not be seen." Here we find that God showed unto Moses His back parts. That means He has a back and shoulders. He has all the different parts of a personal being.

In Genesis 18:3-8, Abraham was talking to God who had not yet revealed His identity.

"And said, My Lord, if now I have found favour in thy sight, pass not away, I pray thee, from thy servant: Let a little water, I pray you, be fetched, and wash your feet, and rest yourselves under the tree: And I will fetch a morsel of bread, and comfort ye your hearts; after that ye shall pass on: for therefore are ye come to your servant. And they said, So do, as thou hast said. And Abraham hastened into the tent unto Sarah, and said, Make ready quickly three measures of fine meal, knead it, and make cakes upon the hearth. And Abraham ran unto the herd, and fetched a calf tender and good, and gave it unto a young man; and he hasted to dress it. And he took butter, and milk, and the calf which he had dressed, and set it before them; and he stood by them under the tree, and they did eat." Here we see that God had all the bodily parts of a man. He had feet which needed to be washed. He had legs which needed to be rested. He had a mouth and digestive tract to eat the meal.

GOD IDENTIFIES WITH MAN

This is the most glorious thing that we could ever realize, that the One who put the universe and worlds into existence is totally identifiable with you and me. That makes me to know that you and I have never known the power that we could get from God—the power of speaking. God spoke worlds into existence; He spoke constellations into existence; He spoke the starry domes of the heavens into existence. He did all this by the word of His mouth. The amazing thing is that we have mouths and we have words and, had we not fallen in sin through Adam, we would have had creativity equal with God. The Lord Jesus is going to redeem us back into a divine relationship with God. We do not know how glorious it is going to be, but we can be sure that the creativity will be there and the similarity will be there. We will see God and understand that He has a spirit and that we have His spirit within us and that we have equal spirits with God.

We will also realize that God has soulical parts and we will demonstrate our soulical parts along with God. Our whole beings will conform to the Almighty and then we shall live and dwell with Him. We will rejoice with Him throughout all eternity.

God the Father has all the qualities of a human being. The Bible substantiates them and especially with the bodily parts. When we cannot see those bodily parts with our natural eyes, it makes some of us believe that He does not have bodily parts. His bodily parts are not related to corporality. They are not related to the dust and minerals that our feet are on here. They are related to what Jesus was when He was transfigured on the Mount and the glory gleamed through the tissues of His skin, and what He was on the day of resurrection. Those are the qualities that God the Father has.

In our resurrected bodies, our total bodily parts will be exactly like the Lord Jesus and like God the Father.

CREATION, NOT EVOLUTION

Science spends millions of hours working on rats and monkeys trying to understand us. That shows you how confused so-called intelligent man can be. When God says "Let us make man in our own image and our own likeness and let us give him dominion," that means man did not evolve, that man did not come up from something else. Man is today as he was from the beginning. Only the devil will put it into anybody's heart to think anything so beautiful as a human person came from anything so ignominious as a small four-footed beast or creature of the earth.

You could believe it the other way, that man dropped off a pedestal and found his way down to where he is today. That might seem to be something to look into, but there is no evidence on the face of this earth that there is anything evolving—nothing at all! They have no proof of anything that is evolving. Even the sun gets darker every day. The sun is actually burning itself out. None of the stars are getting brighter, they are burning themselves out. This shows you that the total universe is a creative act of God. It did not come up, it came down from God out of heaven.

MAN CREATED TO RULE

The magnificent truth is that God created man in his triune being to rule over Planet Earth and everything on this planet. This rulership was to be a function of his spirit. It is not the function of his soulical parts; man was intended to commune with his Maker by his spirit, and to rule this earth through his spirit. This is vitally important because if we do not get this point, we will never understand what the unregenerated man is today. We will have no comprehension of why he is what he is if we do not realize that God created man to live by his spirit and not by his soulical parts.

SATAN ATTACKS

We do not know how long Adam and Eve

may have lived in that garden before the devil
came to him and to his wife and said, "You
don't have to obey God." When he came to
Eve in the garden, he had to deal with the
total trinity of her personality. First he attacked
her body, the weakest part of the human personality. "Hey, woman, look at that fruit. Isn't
it pretty? It is good eating, too. Taste it!"
Next, he said, "You know it will make you
smart?" This was an attack on Eve's soul.
"You want to know something else? You will
be like God." This was his blow against her
spirit. So he hit her body; down she went.
Then he struck her soul; down she went.
Finally he landed a crippling blow against her
spirit. He hit her three ways in the temptation
and she fell all three times defeated—body,
soul, and spirit.

Four thousand years later the same tempt-
er, the devil, met Jesus. After Jesus had
nothing to eat for forty days, he said, "Man,
you're hungry, aren't you? I know how much
power you have; take that stone and make
yourself a nice piece of French bread. It
would taste good with that good crust on it."
Rather than smacking his lips like Eve would
have done, Jesus retorted in Matthew 4:4,
"Man shall not live by bread alone, but by every
word that proceedeth out of the mouth of God."

Satan did not quit there. He took him to the pinnacle of the temple and he said, "You know, for the head of an evangelistic society, you're kind of a poor one. I haven't seen your name in the *Jerusalem Times* at all. You do not have a following. Now if you will jump off of here in front of all these people, they will put that on the front page of the paper. You know the angels will hold you up." Jesus responded in Matthew 4:7, "Thou shalt not tempt the Lord thy God!" Then the devil took Jesus to the third test and he said, "I'll give you all the nations of the world." Satan was thinking, "I could not get your body, I could not get your soul, but if I could get to your spirit..." Jesus said in Matthew 4:10, "Get thee hence, Satan."

It is important to realize that man lives in these three areas of personality, because Satan still attacks just as he did with Eve and Jesus. If we do not defend all three areas of personality, we will not live in the dominion God intended for us. Rather, we will become prisoners of war in Satan's camp.

3

THE DIVINE PURPOSE

God said that on the day Adam ate of the forbidden fruit he would die. Adam ate of that tree, yet his body did not die. It lived 930 years after that, with sons and daughters and grandsons and granddaughters. His soul did not die because his mind remained clear. He could name all the animals and remember their names. He could give a name to every flower on the face of the earth and remember the name of that flower. His emotions did not die, because there was great rage in his family, and one son murdered another son. Adam's emotions must have been very strong—anger, hate, and murder. Man's willpower did not die. Men continued to do as they pleased; they willed not to serve God, and that is what brought the flood. So we see that man did not die in soulical parts. What was it that died?

Immediately when he transgressed, Adam hid from God. Even to this day every sinner hides from God.

THE DAY THE SPIRIT OF MAN DIED

As soon as Eve sinned, she said, "Oh, I'm naked." She was ashamed, and began to look for fig leaves to put them together. Adam and Eve had lost God's presence. They lost what we call the born-again nature. They lost their relationship with God. Their consciences became a second-rate function that they could mess around with and play with and disobey. Beforehand, the human conscience had flowed magnificently and beautifully with God. **It was the third person of the triune being inside of man that died.**

When the spirit of man died, his relationship with God died. When God thrust him out of the Garden of Eden, man was operating in two areas, and not three. He was operating on soul and body. Adam's nature changed from a spiritual being into a soulical being. That is the reason Jesus is called "the last Adam." He brings you back to that very place where man lost his glory and he clothes you again with a glorious robe of righteousness because you have returned to the place where the third part of your being comes alive

in God and you are a new creature in Christ
Jesus. When you come to that place, you
learn how to function there. It will not come
automatically but, if you want to function in
your soulical parts, you can do it.

OPERATING ON TWO CYLINDERS

After their transgression, our forebearers,
Adam and Eve, had two parts—the body and
the soul. That is all you were born with. When
you are born on this earth, you are born with
two parts, not three. You have to be born
again. When Jesus told Nicodemus that, he
could not believe it. Here was an old man,
possibly ninety years old. He was a member
of the Supreme Court in Israel, and a man
that had kept the commandments of God.
Nicodemus loved the young preacher called
Jesus. He came inquiring, "Rabbi, we know
you came from heaven." Jesus did not even
answer him. He simply said, "You must be
born again." Nicodemus questioned, "Now
young rabbi, my mother has been dead quite
a few years and I'm about ninety, what is it
you just said? About this getting born again?"
Jesus said, "There is a birth of the natural
flesh and a birth of the spirit. You must be
born again." Ephesians 2:1 says that you
that were dead in sins and trespasses hath he

revived. In Adam, we have the death of the
human spirit. Man has soulish Adamic mind,
emotions, will, and five senses that in their
natural state will not serve God, do not want
to serve God, and have to be commanded by
the spirit to serve God before they will. That is
the situation that everyone of us are born to
whether we like it or not.

WHO'S ON THE THRONE
OF YOUR SOUL?

Paul says in I Corinthians 15:45, "And so
it is written, The first man Adam was made a
living soul; the last Adam was made a
quickening spirit." So you are two persons.
You have within you the first man Adam. His
blood is in our veins. We also have within us,
as Christians, the last Adam which is a
quickening spirit. Each of your two portions
have a throne. Your soul has a throne, the
throne of your soul is your mind. When a person comes to me and wants to be delivered
from demon power, invariably I have to
relieve that power from his mind. That is the
throne and the devil always looks for a throne.
From the very beginning up in heaven, it was
a throne he was after and even when he has
an antichrist, he'll get a big throne on which
to seat him. He is totally throne conscious.

When he is in hell forever, he will be sitting on a throne down there. Hundreds of people that I have prayed for said it felt like they had bands around their heads. The devil wants to control the throne of the mind. So when I set a person free, I set his mind free first.

THE SPIRIT HAS A THRONE

Man has another throne and that is the throne of his spirit. This is the throne I searched for, for so many years. Where is the throne of man's spirit? It is in his belly. It was Jesus that said in John 7:38, "Out of his belly shall flow rivers of living water." He did not say that it would come out of your head or your heart. He said that out of your belly shall flow rivers of living water. Now God has chosen this little part of your being to establish a throne, and all happiness flows out of there. You cannot laugh really unless it comes from the belly or spirit. You can say, "He-he-he!" but that is from Hollywood and that is tinsel and it is not for real. When you are really happy you laugh, "Ha-ha-ha!" Did you know that when you receive a spiritual language from heaven it flows out of your spirit? No one has ever spoken in a spiritual language to the heavenly Father with his prayer language out of any other place except his spirit. Did

you know when God gave you the gifts of the
Holy Spirit that they flowed out of the belly
area and not the mind area? The nine gifts of
the Spirit all flow from your spirit area. All of
the fruit of the Spirit flows from the belly area.

That new man in you has to become
boss—almost a tyrant. He has to have full
control or otherwise there will be a wild man
running around on the inside of you. When
the spirit becomes king within you and the
rest of you becomes a servant to the king,
then you are a spiritual entity just like Jesus.
You will be living by a new man, by a new
power, and by a new spirit. It will be your
spiritual elements that will be surging up
within you. You will start thinking and it will
not be from your mind; it will be from your
spirit. Your emotions will not flare up and run
away with you.

Did you know that millions of Christians
have no idea whether or not they are living in
the spirit? Did you know that every church
problem that has ever been, was in the
soulish part of the church, the Adamic nature,
and not in Jesus? We must learn to have the
mind of Christ. The mind of Christ was a
spiritual mind, not a carnal mind. Even as a

Christian, you can still live with a carnal mind if you desire. In that case, your rewards in heaven will not be great.

LEAVE NO PLACE TO THE DEVIL

When we lived in Manila, Philippines, one of their number-one movie idols was converted. He had had a stroke. His tongue hung out the side of his mouth and he was almost like an idiot. They brought him to our services where Brother Clifton Erickson was the evangelist. God miraculously healed that man. His tongue went back into his mouth. He got up and began to talk. They brought him in a wheel chair, but he walked out of there as someone else pushed the chair. God had totally healed him. I went to his house to see him. His beautiful wife said to me, "Brother Sumrall, this is not the first time he has had this. He gets this way through his temper. I've seen him scream until he foams at the mouth and falls on the floor." I turned to Carlos and said, "That is your natural Adamic nature. If you ever do it again, you may die." He said, "I promise not to." He was dead in one month's time. His wife said, "Brother Sumrall, he got so angry and he screamed so loudly that people could hear him a city block away. The very moment that

he dropped dead he was bellowing like a bull
and cursing as loud as he could curse."

If you do not get control of that Adamic
nature and subdue it by the power of the
Spirit, it will ruin you and send you to the
wrong place.

4

Human Personality

Until a Christian can differentiate when the soul and the spirit are functioning and operating through him, he will continue to gravitate toward the lower life. He will not be able to rise in the spirit until he knows what it is about. That is why it is so essential to know what is spirit. It is impossible to constantly walk in the spirit if you do not even know what spirit is. The apostle Paul said in Galatians 5:16, "This I say then, Walk in the Spirit, and ye shall not fulfill the lust of the flesh." By "walking in the spirit," he meant walking in God, walking in love, walking in holiness, and not walking in darkness, not walking in sin and rebellion toward God or your fellowman.

THE HOLY SPIRIT ENERGIZES
THE SPIRIT MAN

Romans 8:11 says, "But if the Spirit of him that raised up Jesus from the dead dwell in you, he that raised up Christ from the dead shall also quicken your mortal bodies by his Spirit that dwelleth in you." The Spirit that raised Jesus from the dead is the same power that comes into you to energize you in your spiritual parts. You are going to be quickened while you are living in your mortal body, not just in eternity.

I Corinthians 12:8 says, "For to one is given by the Spirit the word of wisdom; to another the word of knowledge by the same Spirit." These are two of the nine gifts from God, through your spirit. They never come through your mind, your emotions, your will, or your soulical parts.

YOUR FRUIT BETRAYS YOU

In Galatians 5:22, Paul describes the fruit of the spirit. This spirit is your born-again nature that God has put within you. The fruit of that spirit within you (separate from the soul), gives birth to these things. Paul first mentions love. Therefore, you have to ask yourself, "Am I living in love?" The fruit of your human spirit flowing forth out of your total being is love. So now when love does not flow from your being, then you are living in your soul. You know the activities of the spirit by love. If it is hate, or criticism, then it is Adamic. You will die spiritually living in your Adamic nature. You will crush that newborn thing that God has put within you.

Next, the Word of God says that the fruit of the spirit is joy. It has been a very saddening thing to me to find so many Christians that are really not happy. They will tell you that they are not happy. This is a problem resulting from their Adamic nature.

Now the fruit of the spirit life is joy. God wants us to be happy. When you live by your feelings and every little thing that comes around that doesn't suit you makes you unhappy, you're just living for the Adamic nature. If you do not live by Adam, you live by Christ.

Next he lists peace. That comes by being turned on positively, spiritually, and having an appreciation for your fellowman. It just does not come up the other way.

Romans 14:17 says that the kingdom of God is God's righteousness, which is the blood of Jesus Christ shed for you, and it is peace and joy in the Holy Ghost. When you are born again by the Spirit of God and your spirit comes alive, it produces righteousness. God's righteousness covers you and you become right with God, fellowman, and yourself. At the same time when you become right, you become peaceful. If you are disturbed, nervous, and fearful all the time, you are living in your Adamic nature. You are not living by your spirit man.

Paul goes on to list several other attributes of the born-again spirit including such fruit as longsuffering, gentleness, goodness and faith.

5

UNITY AND IDENTITY

We read in I John 5:7,"For there are three that bear record in heaven, the Father, the Word, and the Holy Ghost: and these three are one." The Bible teaches us that man is made up, just like the God-head, of three mighty dimensions. Each is distinct and different. This human structure is actually unique in all the creation of God and all the movements of God throughout the universe. In this creature that we call man we have the apex of all of His creation. We have something completely unique in that man does not have to serve God. Animals have to serve their masters. You can put a lion in a cage and he cannot do a thing about it. God has placed man here to make decisions and to create his own destiny. God wants love and you cannot love unless you have freedom. Prisoners do not have a chance to decide whom they love. Free men can choose whom and what they love. God made man unique in this way.

MADE IN GOD'S IMAGE

Man does have a corporeal body. Beyond that, man possesses a dominant self which is his soul. This is distinct and different from the corporeal body. It is powerful; and it leads and it guides. The soul is a tremendous structure. Born-again people have a tremendous life, a tremendous force, and a tremendous ability called spirit. Why is man a three-fold being, and not four, or six, or eight, or two? Man is made three-fold in every dimension that you find him, three because three is the number of God's divine perfection.

God made man first as spirit. We are a spirit. God is a spirit without corporeality. Demons are spirits without corporeality or a physical being. Man is a spirit that possesses a soul and a body. God made man's spirit to be a king—not a slave. God made man's spirit to rule in his triune personality. The spirit of man must rule; otherwise, the soul and the body will take over dominance and will become kings ruling in their own domain. This would cause the ruin of that personality and alienate it from God and happiness.

When a child is five, or six, or seven years old, if someone can lead him into a spiritual experience, that child grows all of his life on three. What a pity it is for a man to live 50 years, then get saved, and say, "Oh, look how I wasted those 50 years living on two—living in the soul and the body—unhappy, miserable, when I could have been living on three." That is the reason we should win children to the Lord Jesus Christ. That is the reason the Bible says in Proverbs 22:6, "Train up a child in the way he should go." Get him born again. Get the blessing of God in him. Get the anointing of the Lord upon him. Let him know what it means to live in the triune. Let him know that he is three-fold; not two or one. Let him know the unity of his spirit, his soul, and his body, the three elements of the human personality. They can be like a symphony in their movements of loveliness and beauty and music. They can be harmonious without distractions and without having broken hearts.

MAN WAS CREATED TO WORSHIP

In our worship the spirit can be adoring God, praising and magnifying Him, just like the angels before the throne of God in heaven. At

that precise moment the soul or the mind can
be thinking of the beauties of heaven, and of
all the wonderful things that come to us
through Christ. The emotions that belong to
the soul can be in a state of ecstasy with joy
flowing at a higher level than it does regularly.
The will can be in divine submission and
perfect rhythm to God, harmonizing the spirit
and the soul with the will saying, "I like this. I
want this. I'm for this." The same time that
the soul and the spirit are worshiping God,
the body can have expressions of worship.
The head and hands may be lifted in adora-
tion and worship. The eyes can have the light
of heaven in them. The lips can be singing
the praises of God. In this way the total
human personality is in worship.

How many worship services do you attend
where you find that the three parts of you are
not fully functioning? The mind is wandering
off on what it is going to do next week. The
spirit has no part in the place. However, if you
are going to have the perfect man—the ideal
person—there has to be unity and identity.
The spirit has to be doing its function, the
soulical part doing its function, and the bodily
parts doing their functions. The three are
there, but they are united.

DIVINITY OPERATE AS ONE

We must realize that we are exactly as God in heaven. The same thing exists in heaven. The Father, the Son, and the Holy Spirit, counseling in the majestic throne room of God, decided to make man in their own image. This was the movement not of one but of all of them. Genesis 1:26 says, "God said, Let us make man in our image"—God said, "after OUR likeness." Here we see the flowing of more than one.

Matthew 3:16-17, "...he saw the Spirit of God descending like a dove, and lighting upon him: And lo a voice from heaven, saying, This is my beloved Son, in whom I am well pleased." Here we see the divine trinity functioning, operating in divine action. Christ was being baptized in the River Jordan. The Father was speaking from the heavenlies. The Holy Spirit was descending to anoint and to bless the Son as He went forth on His journey through life and upon His occupation on this earth.

The divine trinity made man triune. I Thessalonians 5:23, says, "The very God of peace sanctify you wholly; and I pray God that your whole spirit, and soul, and body be preserved blameless unto the coming of our Lord Jesus Christ." We can see that the born-again person possesses the same component parts which Adam possessed before he fell in the Garden of Eden. We are reinstated.

MAN'S THREEFOLD PERSONALITY

The personality of man is so closely knit that it takes the all-powerful Word of God to even divide the soul from the spirit. Man will never do it. Science will never figure it out. Philosophy will never know what it is all about. They will never have the answers to the reality of what makes a man a spirit and what his soul does and how it functions within him.

THE BODY

Almighty God fashioned the human body from the clay of the earth. Genesis 2:7 says, "And the LORD God formed man of the dust of the ground, and breathed into his nostrils the breath of life; and man became a living soul." Originally there was a close kindred between man and his environment. God did not pick up dust off the moon and make a man down here on the earth. His outer shell is like the earth, the area in which he lives and which he exists.

The body is easy for us to classify and to

identify. Its five senses (seeing, feeling, smelling, touching, hearing) are ever with us. We see that this earthly part of man was not created to be a god or a saviour or a lord or a king. This earthly part of us was created to serve us as a servant, even as a slave. The mortal part of man, the slave, was to obey his spirit part. If the inward man is evil, the carnal clay man will also manifest all the evils of the inward man. If you have lust inside of you, and if you want to hear every dirty thing that you can because there is a spirit of lust within you, that spirit will manifest itself through the clay man. If the inner man is spiritual, the body will demonstrate the fruit of the Spirit. It will be exactly what the spirit wants it to be. That is the outer shell—the human shell.

THE SOUL

Inside the human shell you have the soulish man, or the Adam man. It is full of unspeakable mysteries. Maybe science on this earth will never understand the intricacies of the intellect, emotion, and willpower that combine to make your soul. This part of man is a real self-life, with a close relationship with the outside shell of the body. Your mind, your emotions, and your will live skin-deep, close to the outside of your body. This soul with its three areas helps this body to know what to do, when to do it, and how to do it. God joined the body and the soul together by His breath. He breathed and made the mind, the emotions, the will, and the flesh come alive. He breathed upon them and the two areas flowed together to be subservient to a further area, deeper than those two. Man's body and soul can be good or bad in relationship to the third area, his spirit—his born again nature.

Inside the clay house is a soul, and beyond the soul we find man's spirit. This spirit is as distinct as the other two areas. It is as different as darkness is from light. God gave man's spirit the propensities of communication and communion with Deity which does not belong to man otherwise. Your mind cannot reach Deity. If it could, the philosophers would have all of it, and the uneducated people would have none of it. God said in I Corinthians 1:21, "By wisdom men knew not God."

THE SPIRIT

In his spirit area man was created to be able to communicate with the divine world. Through your spirit you communicate with God. The reason sinners say all kinds of funny things about Christians is because they do not live in the same world. For sinners looking at a Christian, it is like looking into a barrel that is all sealed up and has one little hole. They are on the outside trying to look in and they cannot see a thing, but if you get on the inside you can see everything by looking out. That is how it is when the spirit dwells within you. God gave man this spirit. He gave him a spirit structure within him, that he might understand and know things about God, eternity, and himself.

THERE IS POWER IN UNITY

In this perfect man we see three things. As a body he walks, eats, sees, hears, and feels. He has five senses that God gave him. With his soulical parts he has power over all the animals of the earth. He has power over all the things that live and the vegetation of the earth. Through his soulical parts he rules the natural things that are around about him. He possesses emotions to admire the sunrise, which an animal does not; to admire the sunset, which a beast cannot; to feel real affection and love toward one another. He has the willpower to choose, and to walk as a king on the face of the earth. When he walks in his physical, soulical, and spiritual parts, then he walks with divinity—with God, not with animals and other men. In the evening time

Adam walked with the Most High God. With his spirit he undertakes his limitations and understands what he should do and what he should not do, relative to good and evil. In man's triunity he has a king, a servant, and a slave within him; all three are meshed into one being.

The spirit must exercise his kingship by praising God. Praise brings you into direct relationship with God. If you never lift up your voice and praise God, then this fellowship with God cannot be. In church we should sing joyfully unto the Lord. I have heard the heathen all over the world, and there was not a joyful note. It is mournful; it is death. I have heard the Muslims as they pray out over their foghorns all over their land. How sad and depressing it is.

LET THE SPIRIT BE KING

The Word of God says, "Let the people rejoice!" The beginning of this walk with God is to be sure that the spirit is king. He is your relationship with the Most High. He is your relationship with peace. He is your relationship with joy. He is your divine relationship. Bring Him into focus as the supreme leader of your life by reading the Word, praying, and **worshiping**.

God made man's soul to be a servant. Make your mind be your servant, not your lord. Make your emotions to be your servant. God did not make your emotions for you to get up every morning and say, "How do I feel?" Through your spirit, you are to tell your emotions how to feel. Say, "Emotions, it is time to rejoice!" David said unto his soul, "Soul, why art thou cast down? Rejoice in Jehovah." One David was speaking to another David. The spirit David was speaking to the soul David saying, "Rejoice in the Lord." He commanded himself to rejoice in the Lord. To millions and millions of people their emotions are their king and they live by their emotions. That is the reason for divorces, heartaches, troubles, and all kinds of sorrows. Millions live by their lower nature, by their Adamic nature, or their soulical nature, rather than by the spirit nature and by the Spirit and power of God. God help us to live resourcefully, gloriously, and wonderfully as a united man with a king, a servant, and a slave, living together in one house—our house. In that house, you must know who is lord--the spirit made alive by Jesus. As you walk with Him, talk with Him, and sing to Him, your soulical parts must obey and your physical parts must respond and say, "Yes, I obey."

I ask you to examine yourself and say, "Lord, I am going to make Jesus the king of my life. He's going to put His Spirit in me to guide my life in every way."

CONCLUSION

In the eternalness of God, the body portions of the human are in complete harmony with the human soul and the human spirit forever. What a mighty victory for the Creator God!

In these studies of THE TOTAL MAN we have brought the complexity of the triune human experiment into divine focus. The human person in his born-again experience with the Lord Jesus Christ, possesses a vibrant, living spirit made alive at the New Birth.

John 3:16, "For God so loved the world, that he gave his only begotten Son, that whosoever believeth in him should not perish, but have everlasting life."

Ephesians 2:1-2, "And you hath he quickened, who were dead in trespasses and sins; wherein in time past ye walked according to the course of this world, according to the prince of the power of the air, the spirit that now worketh in the children of disobedience."

We also came to know that man is an immortal soul which consists of mind, emotions, and human will, perfectly coordinated with his spirit.

To our total enlightenment we became acquainted with the corporeal body with five amazing senses which is subject to obey your soul, while your soul is divinely taught and controlled by your born again spirit.

This is divine harmony as the triune God planned it in the counsel chambers of the Trinity at the throne of the Most High.

Let us "Walk in the Spirit, and ye shall not fulfil the lust of the flesh." Galatians 5:16.

MY CHALLENGE TO YOU

If you are not a Christian, I invite you to receive the hope and peace in your heart that only Jesus gives.

To become a Christian, you must deal with Christ Jesus directly. In a quiet moment, bow your head and talk to Him. In your own words say something like this:

"Dear Lord Jesus, I am a sinner. I believe that you died and rose from the dead to save me from my sins. I want to be with you in heaven forever. God forgive me of all my sins that I have committed against you. I here and now open my heart to you and ask you to come into my heart and life and be my personal Saviour. Amen."

If you say that to Christ and mean it, He will come in instantly. At once you will sense you have been transferred from the devil's dominion to the kingdom of God.

Read I John 1:9 and Colossians 1:13. A wonderful peace and joy will fill your soul.

If you pray a prayer like this, let me hear from you. I will send you a little pamphlet entitled, "So You're Born Again!"

Mail your letter to: **Lester Sumrall, P.O. Box 12, South Bend, IN 46624.**

61

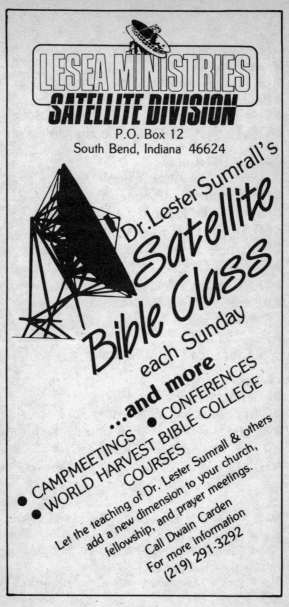

Other books by Lester Sumrall:

□ My payment for $_____ is enclosed
□ CHECK   □ VISA   □ MASTERCARD

_____
SIGNATURE OF CARDHOLDER

_____   _____/_____
INTERBANK NUMBER   EXPIRATION DATE

_____/_____/_____/_____
CREDIT CARD NUMBER

NAME _____

STREET _____

CITY _____ STATE _____

ZIP_____

PHONE NUMBER _____

- -

□ My payment for $_____ is enclosed
□ CHECK   □ VISA   □ MASTERCARD

_____
SIGNATURE OF CARDHOLDER

_____   _____/_____
INTERBANK NUMBER   EXPIRATION DATE

_____/_____/_____/_____
CREDIT CARD NUMBER

NAME _____

STREET _____

CITY _____ STATE _____

ZIP_____

PHONE NUMBER _____

- -

□ My payment for $_____ is enclosed
□ CHECK   □ VISA   □ MASTERCARD

_____
SIGNATURE OF CARDHOLDER

_____   _____/_____
INTERBANK NUMBER   EXPIRATION DATE

_____/_____/_____/_____
CREDIT CARD NUMBER

NAME _____

STREET _____

CITY _____ STATE _____

ZIP_____

PHONE NUMBER _____

24-Hour Prayer Phone
(219) 291-1010